Anna Zhao

Day's Breaking

POEMS

Blue Fishbowl
New York

To My Ancestors, My Family, and D

PREFACE

I have tried many ways to document my life. Diary: It's just too hard for me to keep at it. Photography and videography: I am good at them, but I missed out on some of my most cherished moments. By the time I got my camera ready, the subject had often moved on. Fiction: hiding in stories and between the lines? I prefer something more direct. Then, the high power sent my way - Poetry.

Poetry gives me the maximum freedom. My heart, eyes, ears, nose, and fingers are all lenses, ready to capture a scene. The body is much faster than our conscious mind. It rarely misses. Once my sense organs capture a moment, I can regurgitate it and take my time reproducing it in words.

Of course, reproducing a scene in the most economical and descriptive words can be the hardest part of writing poetry. Mimicking the brilliant works of great poets has been an eye-opening and exhilarating learning experience for me. Edward Lear, Emily Dickinson, Billy Collins, and Naomi Shihab Nye are just a few of the many poets I've learned from this year.

Although the poems are not explicitly time-stamped, their appearance follows a chronological sequence. In these poems, you will feel the change of seasons and the change of mood as time passes. I am naturally optimistic and cheerful, but 2023, in particular, has been a rollercoaster of emotions for me. From heartbreaking sadness to acceptance to gratitude for whatever has come my way, my heart slowly heals and grows stronger.

So, welcome to my 2023 Moments of Life Exhibition. Let me show you around.

CONTENTS

ACKNOWLEDGMENTS

I am grateful to my niece, who inspired my poetry journey, and my family, who support me in everything I do.

I am grateful to D, who believed in and encouraged me to pursue all my artistic ambitions and provided valuable, constructive feedback.

I am grateful to the various organizations that have sustained my passion for languages and written words over the years. Life-changing workshops at New York Writers' Coalition's New York Power Speakers and numerous Toastmasters clubs, Inkwell Shenzhen and its talented members, and NaNoWriMo's July NanoCamp challenge, during which I wrote many of the poems included in this collection.

I am grateful to everyone who crossed paths with me and inspired me. This journey will not be the same without you.

I am also grateful for the Big Bang. To me, everything now is just the aftermath, the ripples from that moment.

Describe A Daily Object

I hate this
Assignment
It's
Too early
Too much salt for an open wound
Yet again
It is never the time
To pick up the little piggy
The ladybug
The bigger piggy
The horse
All the little ones you gave me for good luck
Without tearing my heart apart, again
They live on the desk
Keep me company
When you
No longer

Fish In The Tank

Its mouth is its face
 (Its face is on the top of its head and behind)
No teeth are visible from my angle
It said some
Then it said some more
The mouth opened and closed and repeated
What did you say, I asked

There was absolutely nothing else in the tank
Except for these fish
No seaweed no bubbles no lights - the ordinary pet comforts
So - they are no pets
Maybe some dinner leftovers
Leaving there to die, or
An afterthought
A procrastinated result
A dragging dilemma

The Hooded Crow

I heard
There is a congregation
Every night here
When the world is dark
And humans have disappeared
Into their caves

So I came
To see and admire
How hundreds,
If not thousands of
Raven folks
Have a happy hour
In this Parking lot open bar
In the smoky light of night

Some rubbed their heads together
Some beaks met
Some stood close to each other
Some shared the day's jokes
Except for their clothes
Not much different from humans
All seek some fleeting love
In their fleeting life and in
That fictional, meaningless thing called
Time

Day's Breaking

after Cleo Qian

Day's breaking
Flip over, a blank canvas ready for me
With all the bookmarks from yesterday
How considerate

The day cares not what palette I pick
Bright sunny, or dark grumpy
It hands me the brush
It never rushes
It says, "*feel free.*"
Then waits in silence. Only the birds chirp
And the bullfrogs' mating symphony

How should I paint *today*
A jog at the reservoir to start with?
Till I see
The shimmering lake
The woods' earthly wakening
The long-legged white heron family, and careful!
Better walk around the silver knittings of the black spider

How should I paint *today*
I will stay inside my cocoon
White walls of the empty living room
Sound-proof earplugs
I read NYTimes obituaries
I write unpublished poetry
Drink green tea
Breaking out of black coffee

I daydream on this 9th-floor Balcony, looking down at the sky-blue swimming pool, giant mosaic orchids at its bottom

How should I paint *today*
A black-out nap spell
Then more poetry
When the evening starts to fall, I will get to the Kindergarten on the corner to pick up my niece, a rosy-cheeked flower bud

How should I paint *today*
Dinner at my little sister's?
I was away, for 11 years

How should I paint *today*
I will keep the last stroke short
Just a little into the shadow
For a new day will break
Only a flip away

Love - I

after Czestaw Mitosz

I'm thinking of you
Seven months have passed. We now live in the world's different
corners
You changed your Gmail profile picture today
From our silly laughing to you surfing alone in the sea
I telepathed that man a big red kiss
What an incredible ride we had! I will never forget
The memory that once we were as one did not sadden me
In my heart, I only felt lucky
When New York days are getting longer, I wish you another big blue
summer.

Penthouse

The first bird's dawn song
Turned on the lights in just one

Apartment in the 33-floor building.
That was the penthouse.

I wonder:
They live on the top floor, so they get up early or
They get up early, so they live on the top floor.

My Sister's Guest House

after Billy Collins

I moved
The couch, TV,
Coffee table & everything else
Out of the living room,

That
You kept for
The comforts of
Our parents
When they come to visit.

Forgive me.
The unfilled space is
So easy-going,
And so light.

Pigeons

They are different
From their distant cousins in New York.
They watch me
They are interested
They don't beg for food
They stay out of my reach -
On the high roof of the farmhouse
By the river
Running in the mountains.

Timing Is Everything

after Naomi Shihab Nye

8 AM. I start my day sitting at the desk. Timing is everything.
When the big cup of green tea kicks in, I will be truly ready.

What would be on my way to this moment instead
If I'd pulled myself up when the alarm called repeatedly at 5:30?

We were on the highway back from the city. Timing is everything.
My niece recited a beautiful ancient poem,

"*Let's make a poem of our own*," I said. She agreed and my life started
over.
From there to you reading this poetry book is only a short matter of
time.

I might've stumbled to my face and been crushed by the lunch
hunger tide of high school if not for God knows whose hand
grabbed my wrist that moment, balance restored.
I woke up in the middle of the night and turned my face away when
Julie's brick-thick dictionary fell from the top bunk and hit where my
head was.

What about that tennis ball? Timing is everything.
I turned around to see the ball coming towards me. Something lifted
my right hand to shield my face when the flying green ball hit its
palm and dropped to the ground, bouncing.

Timing is everything; the salsa committee picked that Tuesday over
all other days in the long Summer.
Timing is everything; who designed the sky of that evening? The
most breathtaking Hudson sunset.

If I wasn't sitting alone on that bench where, feet away, you were doing push-ups,
If my date arrived on time - I didn't even remember his name.

But he didn't; I was, and you came over.
"*Wanna dance?*" you asked, and for once, I answered *yes*. Our life-altering story began.

Timing is everything; I was born.
Timing is everything; I met this little town when my craving for New York was fading.

Sensible Woman

Rain in this part of the country
Is like a sensible woman.
She doesn't mix today's problems
With all your wrongs before.
She downpours only from that one specific cloud.
When her point was made,
The entire sky cleared up in an instant,
Like there's never been a dark moment
Between you. So
All you remembered was
Her bright smile.

Markings

In the park, I passed by
A strolling turtle & its walker,
And looked back.

Propping itself up
On the elbows of its strong flippers
The Turtle
Was also looking at me.
Half my height,
Long, elegant neck, and
A tall domed shell with
Golden coin markings.

He is five years old,
Explained its caretaker, who's
Hired by the hour.
Don't eat that! Not clean!
She was now talking to the turtle.
We got to go. It is his apple
Snack time. Her courteous smile.
Meanwhile, the turtle snapped
A few more young grass into
Its mouth.

My googling found out later::
Those markings
Worth
A fortune.

Summertime

In summertime, I saw green treetops above the row houses &
More trees on the hill behind the high-rise.

In summertime, I heard the birds chirping, children cheering and
calling their Mothers, and water splashing in the pool.

In summertime, I touched the bony little claws of the gray parakeet,
who wandered
In through the window & flew straight into my palm.

In summertime, I tasted the bitter taste of green Jasmin tea & like it
still today,
Coffee is no longer a must.

In summertime, I smelt the bracing breeze passing through this
apartment, in from the open Balcony & out through the kitchen side
door.

Don't let this building get in your way, I said.

Mole

To welcome
The newcomer
To its southern turf,
The sun's long finger
Caressed my right cheek,
And just above the lip,
It fire-branded me,
In its own image.

Nap

Black yoga mat
Airy living room
An apartment on the ninth floor
Facing south
In the shades of the valley and the high-rise giants
Is where I nap this Summer
I must be doing something right.
Parakeet sopranos eagerly tweet tweet
From the top branches,
And r-u-m, r-u-m, r-u-m,
Bullfrog baritones rivaled
In the shadowed caves of the pond.
I didn't remember their last notes
When I woke
Clouds rolling in the afternoon blue sky, and
The green hills not so distant
Filled the full frame of the glass balcony

Square dancing

after Georgia Heard

Night after night
These women danced in the square.
Put aside husband, kids, parents, work,
Sweat away all worries on her shoulders,
For a moment
Love this body just for herself.
Night after night
These women danced in the square.

Tip-of-the-tongue

It was ready
Behind the curtain

To make its entrance
When the Emcee calls.

But the aging playbill
Blurred its name.

Stream of Consciousness – I: Lost & Found

Merging into the river

Streetlight around the corner
Broken
Leaning against the hillside,
Hillside Garden, ten-foot-tall red signs
In the river of night
The streetlight broken
The main hall of the Hillside Garden
Brightly lit
A new moon at the corner, too
Helping
Thin stairs leading up to the Hillside Garden signs
Achievable
70 degrees tilt up, but achievable
The green veggies on the menu of the Hillside Garden
Come from the top -
The end of those stairs
The chef walks from Hillside Garden to the veggies growing on the
hillside -
So, achievable
One of these days

The streetlight around the corner broken
Who the hell broke it
The women still came
Music on
They always come
To this corner
The moon too

It was in a mini skirt today
I like its off-white asymmetry gown
But the skirt, yellow gold and cute
When was the first day
These women took up the corner
Someone passing by with a shopping bag in hand
Music too loud, she pointed to the high-rise
The inner circle
Volume turned down
Volume turned up again
Not a defiance

Sweat, sweat, sweat
When was the first day
I came here
I passed by
I joined towards the end
I joined in the middle
I never joined in the beginning
I always join from the middle
Like merging into the highway
Look left, look right
I slide in
No beginning, but I stay till the end
I must see the end

My chest nearly touched the ground
Is the last part push-ups?
The little girl asked her mother
Is the last part push-ups?
You can end it any way you like
I answered her in my mind

Namaste

Finally, the word came back to me
I couldn't fish it out of the river for days, days

Dream – I: Home

Isn't it cruel?
We can't order dreams, can't
Specify where, when & who
The scene tonight we want
To be dropped
Into.

Dream
Is an artistry agency
Specializing in surprise parties. It
Makes its own itinerary &
Draws its own map.

Early this morning
It took me home, maybe so
I can fill in the blank
Left empty yesterday, asked awake
Where was my home?

One side of the house opened
To a small alley
Some tall stools, then
A long, tall table, behind
the window to a room where
Slow blues & soft lamplight
Steaming out.
To the table's left
Were a few umbrellas
In the rack
For the regulars
Of this open-air bar or

Whoever passes by.

My heart feeling warm.

I waited in the empty alley.
No blink because
At any moment
The host may step
Into the room
To serve a drink.

When I'd see you -
My longed home.

Bullfrogs

Eat spiders, scorpions,
Rodents, snakes,
Birds, fish,
Other frogs, and
Just about anything else
That passes in front of them.

I wondered what
These two giant bullfrogs ate today
Before laying naked on my chopping board.

My Breasts

Twin sisters
Neighbors back-to-back
A finger's distance apart
Never across.

One night
The one on the left, l-o-n-g craned her neck,
To meet the one on the right
Eye-to-eye. I woke up
In a cold sweat.

Moment of Peace

after Wendell Berry

When worries about the future creep up on me again,
I hear their teeth sinking into my heart,
My breath held, my pulse wildly beat,
I go wash the undone dishes in the sink,
Until everything is sparkling and shining on the draining rack.
I go sweep the floor, sweep every corner of the apartment,
Until all the dust, the fallen hairs, has been cleared.
I go do laundry, iron and fold,
Return them to their regular place in the closet, by category by color.
I make sure my last conversation with anyone
Ends with a warm temperature.
Then I come
Into a moment of peace
Knowing all loose ends are tidied up, and am ready
For whatever comes next.

Word Of Mouth

The moment I opened it
To shield the sun, which
Even in the Greenway
Lined by trees
Is too much for the human skin,
Each move of the dark green umbrella
Was being
Watched,
Broadcasted,
Warned about,
Stood guard against,
From bird to bird,
All the birds,
Now the whole damn woods.

Under the umbrella, I felt
Slightly offended.

Ode To The Moth On The Wall

After Joyce Kilmer

In a 7/11 Cafe
I sat and saw
A sleeping moth
On the snow-white wall.

Oh, little moth on the wall
Who made your heavenly evening gown?
Nothing I've seen like it around.
It is the jewel in the crown.

Lush dark brown velvet
Lines of purest white artfully adorned
Wide and full flows the grand skirt
Under your tight princess line hugged waist.

Oh, little moth on the wall
How can you be so unflawed?
The symmetry, the splendor of all
Impeccably echoed to the details infinitesimal.

Oh, little moth on the wall,
To a mortal, the divine you revealed!
I can attempt mediocre poetry,
But a masterpiece like you, only Designer Almighty can create.

Location, Location, Location!

Two square dance circles
In the neighborhood:
One on the street corner,
One near the river.
No more than hundreds of yards apart,
But most people
choose the former.
One must come early
To secure a spot.

I've tried both
Before joining the corner group.
I am no match
For the mosquitos from the river.

Dream – II

Head spinning,
Like just off somewhere I was thrown.
Where am I now?
A moment ago, you were carrying me on your shoulder
Then you realized the game I was playing.
I giggled, hot spring in my blood trickling
Not hot, just the right amount of warmth
The type of -- only you and I exist in the world.
You put me down after I tapped on your right shoulder
Not coldly not abruptly, a gentleness in the right amount.
Somehow I knew you should be somewhere else
Some work to be done
Time to say goodbye.
You turned around to face me,
So tall as you were in real life,
And kind eyes - not rushing, you take your time -
As they could be in ideal conditions
Where we could be, still together.
We locked eyes,
You smiled, you waved
I must have done the same - which
Must have disrupted the dream.

Bark

after Billy Collins

A tree's cemetery on the outskirt
Graves harden into shields
Safeguarding the young, the living inside

Or the reason,
I take long detours,
Whenever I see a mean dog

We Might Be Wrong About Evolution All Along

after Billy Collins

Early humans
Early victors
Early conquerors
How do you feel
To see your heirs' vegetarian diet
When way back then
You feasted on meat as the apex predator?

Love – II

You saw me
So I existed
Spotlighted
Against the pitch-black
Universe behind

Two foldable sticks on each side
Attached to a central cylinder
This is my body
Under that thing
looking down at it
Called my head

Not much of a look
I guess
But for me
The best highlight
From nothing
My humble beginning

I am blue; I am yellow
I am rainbow colored
Your eyes told the fairytale
I took your word
because in it
I was so beautiful

Without warning
You shut your eyes
To illuminate
Must be tiring

No! ———
I screamed in the dark
but it was not a decision
Up to
the imagined

Back to nothing
My humble beginning
my humble ending

I Will Wait Then.

Overnight Parking

The balcony safety grills park overnight flights.

Once, there was a dragonfly.
Then a pair of green lacewings - a pair!
A muscular wasp with unknown last name,
And early this morning, a big fly.

It hung on a steel wire upside down.
For a while, we listened together
The white-collared green bird
Singing its dawn song…

Spotting me, the fly pilot turned upright.
Its giant headlight eyes on alert, brightly red.
Then a flash of its beating wings, then I blinked
Then it was gone.

A Villanelle: A Male Garter Snake Flicked His Forked Tongue

I flick left, I flick right
Omnipotent compass long
Take me to my dinner & my bride

The afternoon sun shines
Time to make some rounds
I flick left, I flick right

Underlining the goldmines
The compass shows me its magic found
Take me to my dinner and my bride

A family of juicy mice of eight or nine
The patch of lawn, their nighttime playground
I flick left, I flick right

I'll chill behind the tree till moonshine
When the sweet baby mice scuttle & bounce
Take me to my dinner and my bride

I won't let you wait long, my Valentine
See you in the next town, keep your perfume on
I flick left, I flick right
Take me to my dinner and my bride.

Sonnet 22

after William Shakespeare

My glass does not persuade me I am old.
Grains of salt in anyone's claim, why not glass?
Besides, glass is plenty in this household.
Which one and when is a matter of maths.
The bathroom mirror is best for the night
Under dim light when my skin's a soft glow.
The living room one was for day. Sunshine
Behind, a silhouette hasn't much to show.
Also, I can't grow old, truth be told. My
Man used to say, *Stop acting like a child.*
You will always be five. Then his goodbye.
The best boy in man I can ever find.
I live now in shards of the world he left -
Forever childlike per his loving spell.

A Pantoum: 56 vs 112

I pondered over the numbers.
Sinead O'Connor, the singer, died at 56 yesterday.
She was the new row in my death stat table.
I am figuring out who died young and who lasted long.

Sinead O'Connor, the singer, died at 56 yesterday.
For a few hours, she topped the NYTimes obituaries.
I am figuring out who died young and who lasted long.
She was interesting alive as well as when she was gone.

For a few hours, she led the NYTimes obituaries.
Then somebody new took her place.
She was interesting alive as well as when she was gone.
Turning a corner, the line behind her was getting long.

Then somebody new took her place.
Julian Berry, the playwright, died at 92 in his sleep.
Turning a corner, the line behind her was getting long.
Most July voyagers crossed the 70th milepost.

Julian Berry, the playwright, died at 92 in his sleep.
If you think he was the oldest, you'd be wrong.
Most July voyagers crossed the 70th milepost.
Not for a surgery infection, Louise Levy, a lady of 112, would have
lived on.

If you think he was the oldest, you'd be wrong.
Beverly Moss Spatt, Richard Barancik, and Johnny Lujack almost got
to 100.
Not for a surgery infection, Louise Levy, a lady of 112, would have
lived on.

Her daughter remembered her, *"she was sugar and spice and everything nice."*

Beverly Moss Spatt, Richard Barancik, and Johnny Lujack almost got to 100.
Ms. Levy loved Tai Chi, Bridge, and knitting sweaters for hospitalized babies.
Her daughter remembered her, *"she was sugar and spice and everything nice."*
I pondered over the numbers.

The Night Sky

after Karen Downs-Barton

To my west, the Sun had dipped below the horizon.
We will meet again in twelve hours if all goes well.
The sky pulled up its blue blinds,
Let seen the curved dark space I was sailing in.
But the stars still found me with their nocturnal eyes,
Peering from near and far.
Already in mid-air
Was the moon. I again
missed it - its leaping out of the eastern horizon.

Carrying me on its back, the Earth runs onwards and spins.

My dipping below the western horizon was not missed
By the moon, it was
Already in mid-air.
I peered at the stars near and far.
I have no nocturnal eyes, but I was still found.
I was sailing in the curved dark space
Let seen when the blue blinds of the sky were pulled up.
If all goes well, we will meet again in twelve hours.
To the east of the Sun, I rise from the horizon.

Comedy

I fell in love with Mr. Bean,
His storytelling body spellbound -
A sculpture sculpted, and gone, in real-time.
The young tabby cat pounced on his prey,
Grab it, toss it, catch it again, bite it, kick it…
And his prey, a large curled-up leaf that fell off a tree.
Bravo, cat Don Quixote!

If My Little Sister Writes About Me

She came to this world to play,
To do what she feels like.
I came to this world to work,
To do what I feel I should.

What Is Love?

The squirrel mother can't count.
She doesn't know
How many babies she had in total.
She took them in her mouth,
One at a time, to a new nest,
After the raccoon's visit.
When she came back for the last time
She thoroughly checked:
Under the leaves bed
In all corners
Then the outside
The top of the nest
The sides, the backside
The underside.
She was to make sure
None of her babies would be left behind.

Side by side

I tried to find an alone leaflet
On the Wild Senna stems. There

Wasn't any. Each leaf has a sister
Or brother by its side. Their

Thoughtful mother had it all
Evenly planned out. The

Veins on each blade make
A string of green hearts. Nowhere

A sharp corner. Smiles are prescribed
By these little natural therapists.

Zen

after Emily Dickinson

No weather, no seasons,
No air pressure, no flow,
No change of temperature,
Stuck in early Summer, forever.
Ah! What a boring place!

Mirage

In the thick fog of
Crystal-clear
Reality
I close my eyes
To see
The way ahead

The Flood

The piglets
Scuttled around on
Their little feet. The
Crate bars are too high
To stop them yet.

Their mothers each
Stood in their
Metal cage, locked,
Their feet buried underwater.
And the flood

Kept rising.

Life's Fair

after Gwendolyn Brooks

Life's fair. Life
For share. Life

Is now. Life
Takes plow. Life

Is act. Life
Runs fast. Life

Is fun. Life
Waits none.

Seed

I began as a seed.
The seed grew.
Till it was too big,
The pod popped.
I fell off the mama tree.

Barley tea

No one was home.
I reached to touch
The ceramic cup's white body
On the kitchen table
Expecting cold. But
It was warm.
The golden barley tea.
So my sister was just here!
Instantly,
I felt the house's beating pulse.

My Little Sister

We started at the same place, Mama's womb,
Seven years, seven months, 14 days in between,
I remembered, the day she came home,
The Sun shone in from the left window. The room was bright and
quiet.
She was lying alone on the bed, a tiny bundle
Big dark eyes. I had no clue what to make of it,
For a long time.

We jogged today side by side, on the reservoir's
Winding path, the first time in our lives, when my dark hair
Was turning gray, & that little bundle now had a child of her own.
I still have no clue what to make of it, being an older sister and all
that.
I just led the way, taking patient steps, setting an example, setting
One example,
She ran her own way. From time to time,
I look back, to check on her.

Overspill

To boost my immune system,
The doctor gave me
Vitamin B & E.

I did pull-ups on a thick
Branch of a tall tree
Effortlessly
In my dream.

When I woke up
The grin was still
On my lips.

The Shooting

It took me a full second
To wake from the daze
Of staring into the
Dark Throat of a gun,
Training on me, on my face.
He pulled the trigger
The moment I realized it,
It being I was shot by a gun.
- Where did the bullet go?! -
The mind was busy figuring
As the body already pressed on
To the staring muzzle
& the person behind it.
Did you point at me?
My eyes, loaded pistols. Firing ready.
I was pointing at the tree, I… I am sorry.
His trembling voice. A boy of
Eight-ish years old with large
Eyes, and the Simulation toy
Of an M416 assault rifle.
OK. My cold gaze seized him
A moment more, before
I passed him on the right and continued my way.
He knew he was forgiven.
A bullet-speed lesson.

Habit

As I crouched down behind the riverbank fence
to prepare the camera
The great Heron had faded once again
Into the sky.
Not heard or seen its wings flapping
Or known to which way it went.
Just like every time before
It does not take any chance
On humans, a typical chance animal.

Rush hour

Cloud commuters,
The heavyweights & little guys
In varying shades of gray
Rolling south
For their next gig,

When humans in
Varying sizes of cars
Heading north,
Like a strange beetle,
With a long body and thousands of legs,
Barely moving.

Dream - III

I was propelled upwards,
Into the air,
Like a pebble from a slingshot.
Now I am higher than
The tree that awed me, then
More trees under my feet,
Then the whole mountain
Was beneath me. I saw its
Entire body, all its past trailing
Behind it, and its beginnings.

Trapped Praying Mantis

My hand chased it
From one white tile to another
On the kitchen wall -
A green body made it easy.
Its bulging eyes fading out
Their last tinge of red,
To green, the daylight mode.

Now, he is caught
Between my fingers.
Its body so soft
I barely feel it
Except the numbing tinglings,
That's him fighting me with all
His blades and spikes.

My hand unfurled slowly
To put him on the balcony railing when
He surprised me,
Soaring to the sky.
I can almost hear him laughing.
Rapid wings flitting
Like Green propellers.

End of Summer

Dim front desk
Locked entrance to the pool
Too late!
Doorman's pitying news and
We came in swimming suits.

The Summer here
Had officially ended – Yesterday
On August 31st.
New calendar filling rules learned only after, and
Our barely used gym card.

Not even a goodbye.
…

Very well then.
We crossed the street.
It was a good dinner.

Bewildered

The wide-eyed street kitten
Looked up at me
And meowed for help.
A dozen or more
Giant African snails
Circled at her feet.

I don't know exactly
What help she seeks:
To learn how a cat eats snails, or
How a cat fights off
The siege of a snail army?

Naked

It is said
One-third of our lives
Spent asleep in bed.

So I sleep
Bare body
Bare neck
Bare nails too
Every night.

So that no shred
Of bother bore
To the other side.

Mom & Daughter Under The Streetlight

after Alasdair Mac Mhaighstir Alasdair (translation: Taylor Strickland)

You are not a good mom!
And tears, from the little girl.
Quicksilver, droplets splashed.
I don't want you to be my mom anymore!
More splits, she blew harder.
Droplets' metallic skin, blocking heat
Widened the crevasse.
As dark and silent
As questions and played back moments over
And over.
Breath held.
Breath let go.
The woman rose.
Scooter started, waiting for the passenger
Homebound, quicksilver
Rejoined, one whole sphere.

Turf

The waves kept tight tabs on
The acres to their name on Earth.

The waves knocked down
The trespassers, the human things

The so called Reclaimed land- Did we approve it?
The waves asked.

Elusive Birds

To all off-grid creatures

Hard-to-track
Is an ancient art, though
Harder and harder still
When tens of thousands of
Satellite eyes
Search for you
From the sky
At any time
That's why
My feathered friends
You must learn new skills
Become Houdini!
Become the best
Escape artists
You can be
When you need
To get out of
Traps, nets, ropes, chains,
Cages, trackers, guns, bullets,
Camouflages, binoculars, tranquilizers,
Human prying eyes, filthy fingers, greed, more greed,

Keep hiding, please.

The Swinging Swing

A pendulum rocks
From side to side.

No one's fault. I am
Only a flash in its passing.

My face today & tomorrow
Someone or something else.

Anthurium – I

after Ted Kosser

Caring for a houseplant
Is not my thing.
I once returned a leather laptop sleeve
Of a well-known brand because
It took more than five seconds to put the laptop in,
I told the sales rep,
Who chuckled first before realizing it was not a joke and asked
How much time you allow for it?
None, I said.
In the end, I bought a hard-shell plastic case.
It was perfect, as clear as quiet.

Thus I moved in, thus ended
The privileged lifestyle
Of my flamingo flowers roommate.
Out of human's shabby cave!
Live in the glory of nature! To them I hailed.
On the Balcony, they
Bathe the direct Sun
Drink fresh rainwater
Just like a time once upon they were
In the far, far away rainforest.

All was well except
Their blood-red heart-shaped leaves
And their once bright yellow spikes
Slowly turned green.
O! An entirely green anthurium!
O! My genius Frankenstein monster!
O! My eagerly growing guilt!

Secret Wish

Make no mistake, I love my eyes.
They are small and very near-sighted,

But without them, things would be much
Worse and dark. Yet still,

I secretly wish for an upgrade
So that the indifferent see-through space

In front of me, above me, and around me,
Be differently labeled and color-scaled so that

So that I can tell the different species in there:
nitrogen, oxygen, argon, carbon dioxide and

The water vapor, and tell how they were feeling –
Whether any of them had had enough

So that I could have ve chosen another day to do laundry;
I could have avoided hanging out the clothes

In the morning only to find
They were still soaking wet when the sun had set.

Autumn Day

after Rainer Maria Rilke

Hints of cooling in the wind
Dawn grass' little shivering
Leaves drifting down in their yellow gowns
Sleep under a blanket

Autumn announced its arrival
In many ways
But the surer way
For me
Is your birthday
When
The Sun
Makes midway
Of its run
Across the poles.

Tomorrow
It is
A longer night.

Wild Again

Merely days ago, it felt like,
This place was frighteningly big
Lost things cast around
Their shadows.

And now, it is filled full and fit
The long tentacles of the octopus
Inside were let loose, Stretched omnidimensional.

Her space, redefined.

Morning Shopping

The supermarket was packed on Saturday morning.
Supplies brimmed over to the outside, boxes
Of vegetables and bubbling live seafood.
The tabby cat didn't buy much and saved a plastic bag.
Before he disappeared into the bush,
I saw a shrimp's swinging tail.

After Lunch

Take a siesta,
Hanging low, eyelids heavy:
The cloud mother, full-figured
Surrounded by her sleeping cloud babies,
One here, one there, another one not far.
Their breathing so soft
No stir in the still
Blue sky sea.

A Snapshot

after Thomas McGrath

Dusk in the valley was nothing fancy, a dimming sky.
Deserted business quarter, except for one
Small shop with the "Closed" sign, but
Its glass doors objected to none neighborly eyes.

 Office desk by day was now the dining table.
Woman sat tall, picking up vegetables from the plate into her bowl
and listening.
The man, nodding, his back to the door, sat on a small stool like a
child.
Between them, the boy, laughing, gesturing, telling
His story probably of his school day.
Rule of thirds. A complete picture.   Parents, kid, and their livelihood.
All here. All together.

Declutter

I tossed all the Shoulds to the corner.
To be shredded.
They are for the *ideal* humans in *ideal* conditions.
I am neither.

I stuffed the Past Tenses into a box:
Argued, cried, shouted, missed, and all their related.
To the landfill, they are headed.
Old styles for old days,
No more relevant.

So much space freed!

I give some to the Present Simples:
Jog, Write, Listen, Cook, and their close circles.
Trendy styles for an active life,
Essentials to keep.

The largest space I save for the Present Continuous.
Attach the ING magic hook to a Present Simple,
Sing-ing, Danc-ing, Touch-ing, Feel-ing, Lov-ing…
Voila!
I am the dazzling happening!

The Parade

There were five chicks. One went missing.
Now there are four.

Their wings are just forming.
Two chicks wore red young combs—future roosters.
They look ahead when their little claws scratch the soil for worms.
This formation of flowing shapes led the parade, heading east.

Following behind were the toddlers. Limbs growing.
They were followed by their mothers.
On the side was the woman who walked the chicks every morning.

Also following the chicks were many eyes
In the bushes wayside:
The hunting cats were waiting for the right time.
One of them saw the last of the missing chick.

Mr. Black

after Edward Lear

Mr. Black, the houseless cat,
Had stopped cursing me
With his raspy voice.
Even that
He figured out
Won't get me
To bring him food.
      Him food!
      Him food!
I forgot again to bring him food!

Not a Gray Strips, or a Short Bang,
Mr. Black is not into gangs.
Tail up straight, he patrols the compound,
Gate to gate.
Under the dome, everywhere is home.
Nothing beats unattached freely roam.
      Freely roam!
      Freely roam!
Life is sweet to freely roam!

One of the tabby sisters gave birth.
Two mini tabbies and two are soot black
From root to the tip of fur.
Everybody can see
Who is their dad.
      Their dad!
      Their dad!
Mr. Black, the old bachelor, is their dad!

Sometimes we just looked at each other,

His jade green eyes, his chin on paws.
Two wandering islands
Let it drift

Ghazal: Lost Again

after Mimi Khalvati

I assumed this was the right turn. But I am lost again.
Like all the times before, I was lost again.

A happy river running,
The Sun sprinkled its glimmers over and over again.

White herons fly over the dancing river,
Tiny workboats headed north, but turned back again.

You don't focus! you used to say,
I guess you can say that again.

But like every time before, I don't regret
Getting lost and getting lost once again and again.

For that's how - I run into this river, run into that long wall of poems
& read them all,
And how I run into you. I'll keep getting lost till we can find each
other again.

A Brown Ox

Grazed the green
Grass on the berm in
The middle of the
Road. On both sides,
Cars whizzed by
At 40 km per hour.

Shanghai – I: Her Best Age

The woman carries herself well.
Gentle edges of the face
No make-up, but
Lots of work to look this way these days.
Her hair neatly pulled back
Into a low bun.
Soft waist,
Rippling hemlines of the skirt
Around her ankles.
She was quiet,
All you hear is her light footsteps.
That
Is this city,
In her middle-aged years
Maybe her best.
She is not shy,
Meeting your gaze, and
Drowning you
In her misty smile.

Shanghai - II: Between The Lines

Everywhere was clean, at every moment.
Everyone was polite to everyone else, the cars gave me more than
enough time to cross the street.
Everything was so pleasantly quiet: the traffic, people living on their
phones and in their own minds, not a sound of honking.

But why, why
Under her perfect jawline,
I heard a silent sigh.

Shanghai - III: The Young Man And The River

Fingers, his hands of long fingers covered his
Eyes' color unseen, but I can guess. His dark
Tired bike and dark tired clothes. On the
Keystone, top of the bridge, the young
Man stood upright, facing the
River running towards his covered
Gaze will fill up again with the morning
Green, the green that he remembers and holds on to.

Shanghai - IV: Fishermen

Barely six o'clock, they'd lined up the river -
Guys with salt-pepper hair,
Lures, hooks, reels, rods,
Buckets, and they must I am sure, mosquitos permit.
I jogged by, light.

On the river's other side
Was another fishing squad,
Eight or nine-night herons, in their black cap and cloak.
They came bare-handed, just a stubby body power-posed:
Yellow feet wide apart, wings on hips, chin up, and laser-focused
eyes,
Little white bellies shone off the dark green water.

Quack! Quack!
The one hovering to land was warned, and
Greeted with morning cold pecks.
Slowly…
Turf and silence slowly
Resettled.

Who'll go home today
With a full load?

A Zoom Meeting

Outside Z's window, the night was falling,
While on my side, the Day's rising high.
Like a seesaw in slow-motion.
The world turns
On the pivot that Archimedes desired.

Littering

A small black berry rolled into the middle of the road
Overhead, the sky shrugged.
Looked to the side, branches of the camphor tree
Trembling, birds departed and arriving
Flycatchers, Tufted Titmouses, and Thrushes with white brows
All were served.
Hard-to-please gourmets, they spat out the ones not pass.
At my feet, dark purple spins.

A Haiku: Dog Floppy

He stayed with the gym
Then the spa, no lasting home
his grin and charm trot

A Prayer

Almighty universe.
I know
I am in your hands.
I am in good hands.
The only hands I am in.
The hands I cannot not be in.
I used to think,
I was in my own hands. But my hands are so small, so desperately
frail.
Then I see, behind mine are your hands.
They lifted me
To all the places I could be.
I no longer make plans like I used to: daily, weekly, monthly, 5-year
10-year vision.
Now, my vision only goes so far
To the end of this moment.
The moment YOU planned for me.
I am waiting to see
All the plans YOU Have for me,
In the show, I am the hero, but the plot was by you.
And I know
You'll always surprise me.

Self Portrait

after Chen Chen

With electricity, with Zoom, with the worldwide web flowing through my stop, with enough money to buy today's breakfast, lunch and supper, with no debt, I claim every penny in the bank under my name, with a roof over my head and a rental so I don't worry about its future, with enough clothes to keep me warm in this sharp cold front, with new toe socks hat don't slip off my heels, with pants so comfortable I don't even feel I was wearing them, with an iPhone 8 plus, the model I took pain to find, just so I can feel the Home button when I press it, with warm water to drink before the workshop, so my teeth can stop chattering, with pen and notebook by my side, the blue ballpen, only 1 and half local bucks, but it is so light, I write sometimes just because of it, with morning touching the ground, unfolding, red carpet rolled out for me to do whatever, with no commute to make, I can stay put before this desk, open a book, with knowing my niece was getting out of bed to school, with knowing all my loved ones are starting their day or evening as usual, doing their routines, nothing out of the ordinary at the moment, with my pumping heart, with this piece finished.

ABOUT THE AUTHOR

Anna Zhao holds 3 business degrees and has worked as a financial specialist for industry companies, academic institutions, and non-profit organizations.

But words and languages are Anna's true passion. She published an animal tale in a children's story magazine in grade school, won prizes in newspaper essay contests, and wrote praised business-themed ebooks for clients. Since 2018, she has been writing at the New York Writers Coalition. Some of her work is included in the anthology Common Unity: Writing From NY Writers Coalition Workshops. Anna lived in New York City for nearly a decade.

From the end of 2022, Anna devoted herself to her beloved words and began writing poetry. She currently lives in Guangdong, China, close to her sister's family and their two native English-speaking tuxedo cats.

WORKBOOK SERIES

The "Workbook" series is the poet's annual poetry collection, published at the end of each year starting in 2023. This series testifies to the poet's continuous learning commitment from other poets, humans, animals, and all authentic and inspiring life forms.

www.ingramcontent.com/pod-product-compliance
Lightning Source LLC
LaVergne TN
LVHW021409080426
835508LV00020B/2516